The Supermarket

by Gail Saunders-Smith

Content Consultant:
Courtney Cain
Manager, Information and Education Services
National Grocers Association

Pebble Books
an imprint of Capstone Press

1

Pebble Books

Pebble Books are published by Capstone Press
818 North Willow Street, Mankato, Minnesota 56001
http://www.capstone-press.com

Library of Congress Cataloging-in-Publication Data
Saunders-Smith, Gail.
    The supermarket/by Gail Saunders-Smith.
        p. cm.
    Includes bibliographical references and index.
    Summary: Simple text and photographs depict a trip to a supermarket, covering the workers and the areas inside.
    ISBN 1-56065-776-6
    1. Supermarkets -- Juvenile literature. [1. Supermarkets.]
    HF5469.S27 1998
    381'.148--DC21   98-12127
                                                      CIP
                                                       AC

Note to Parents and Teachers

This book serves as a visual field trip to a supermarket, illustrating and describing the various workers, areas, and equipment. The close picture-text matches support early readers in understanding the text. The text offers subtle challenges with compound and complex sentence structures. This book also introduces early readers to expository and content-specific vocabulary. The expository vocabulary is defined in the Words to Know section. Early readers may need assistance in reading some of these words. Readers also may need assistance in using the Table of Contents, Words to Know, Read More, Internet Sites, and Index/Word List sections of the book.

2

Table of Contents

4

A supermarket is a large store. People buy food at supermarkets. They put the things they want to buy in grocery carts.

Fresh foods and frozen foods are in departments. Departments are places in a supermarket. Each department has a different kind of food. Some foods come in cans, jars, and boxes. These foods are in aisles.

Fresh fruits and vegetables are in the produce department. Workers stack fruits and vegetables in piles. They check each piece. They make sure the foods are safe to eat.

Milk and butter are in the dairy department. The dairy manager checks the dates on the cartons. The manager makes sure all the foods are safe to eat or drink.

Ice cream and pizza are in the frozen foods department. Workers keep the freezer cases full. They wear gloves to keep their hands warm.

14

Fresh beef, chicken, and pork are in the meat department. The butcher cuts and weighs the meat. Then the butcher wraps the meat in plastic. This keeps the meat fresh and safe to eat.

Bread, cakes, and cookies are in the bakery department. The bakers also make pies and rolls. They put frosting on some cakes and cookies.

Cans, jars, and boxes of food are in aisles. Each kind of food has its own place on a shelf. Boxes of cereal are in one aisle. Cans of vegetables are in another aisle.

People pay at the checkout counter. The cashier moves packages over a scanner. The scanner tells the cashier how much something costs. The checkout counter is the last stop at a supermarket.

Words to Know

aisle—a path between two rows of shelves

butcher—a person who works with fresh meat

cashier—the person that people pay when they buy things

checkout counter—the place in a store where people pay for the things they buy

dairy department—the place in a supermarket that has milk, cheese, butter, and other items; coolers in the dairy department keep foods cold

freezer—a cooler that keeps foods so cold that they become hard; freezers keep foods from becoming rotten or bad to eat

fresh—something that has not been cooked, dried, or frozen; also something that has not become rotten or bad to eat

frosting—a sweet sugar coating used to decorate cakes, cookies, and baked goods

frozen—something that is cooled until it is hard

fruit—a piece of a plant that people eat; fruit tastes sweet

grocery cart—a large basket on wheels that people use as they shop

scanner—a machine that uses a beam of light to read prices on packages

spoil—to rot or become bad to eat

vegetable—a piece of a plant that people eat; vegetables usually do not taste sweet

Read More

Hautzig, David. *At the Supermarket.* New York: Orchard Books, 1994.

Repchuk, Caroline. *My Little Supermarket.* Brookfield, Conn.: Millbrook Press, 1997.

Ripley, Catherine. *Do Doors Open by Magic? and Other Supermarket Questions.* Toronto: Owl Books, 1995.

Internet Sites

Welcome to Our "Virtual Home Town" Grocery Store
http://www.geocities.com/Heartland/Hills/8618/grocery.html

The Grocery Store Project
http://www.ualberta.ca/~schard/grocdc.htm

Mathland: The Grocery Store
http://ericps.ed.uiuc.edu/npin/respar/texts/helping/math/grocery.html

Index/Word List

Word Count: **263**
Early-Intervention Level: **14**

Editorial Credits
Lois Wallentine, editor; James Franklin, design; Michelle L. Norstad, photo research

Photo Credits
Barbara Stitzer, cover, 1, 4, 6, 8, 10, 12, 14, 16, 18, 20

24